WITHDRAWN

THE WHITE STALLION

THE WHITE STALLION
and Other Poems

BY GUY OWEN

JOHN F. BLAIR, Publisher
Winston-Salem, N. C.

*The woodcut on the title page
is by Ann Carter Pollard*

PRINTED IN THE UNITED STATES OF AMERICA

BY HERITAGE PRINTERS, INC., CHARLOTTE, N. C.

For my father and mother

Acknowledgments

The author is grateful to the editors of the following publications for permission to reprint poems which first appeared in their pages: *American Weave, Bitterroot, Envoi, Epos, Flame, Florida Education, Folio, Green River Review, Impetus, Kaleidograph, Kauri, New Orlando Anthology, Patterns, Poetry, Poetry Florida, Poetry Review, Poetry South-East: 1950–70, South, South and West, Southern Poetry Review, Southern Poetry Today, Tennessee Poetry Journal, The Carolina Quarterly, The Hawk and Whippoorwill, The Lyric, The New England Review, The New York Times, The New York Tribune, The News and Observer, The Poet, The Saturday Review, The Snowy Egret, The Stetson Review.*

A number of these poems appeared previously in *Cape Fear Country* (1958) and *The Guilty and Other Poems* (1964) and have been revised for the present collection.

The author also wishes to express his gratitude to Appalachian State University for an appointment as Writer-in-Residence (Fall, 1968), which made this book possible.

Contents

I

Cape Fear Poems

My Father's Curse

My father strode in anvil boots
    Across the fields he cursed;
His iron fingers bruised the shoots
    Of green; he stabbed the earth.

My father cursed both sun and rain;
    His sweep cut corn and weed,
And where his fiery plow had lain
    The ruined earth would bleed.

Yet though he raged in bitter brew
    Thick oaths that belled his throat,
God rammed His springing juices through
    And fleshed Himself in fruit.

The Old Men
(Thoughts of a Young Girl)

Why do they never speak, the old men,
Leaning behind banisters when I pass?
Staring from rotten porches, they rock,
Dry sticks between thin legs,
Drooling snuff. I see their naked tongues,
Lizard eyes that gulp me in the heat.

Or at stores, hunkered on blue salt licks,
Their brittle fingers shake, fumbling at flies.
They grin. Why will they never speak?

I never look back, once gone—
But feeling their eyes on me like a stain,
My flesh shrinks close to the bone.

Deserted Farm

I took a walk through woods and snow
Until I came to a garden row
Gone to sedge, then a gate of boards
Rotting beneath two martin gourds.

A roofless shed, an old turn plow
Said men were here, but not here now.
"Where have they gone?" I asked the pump
Rusting beside the light'ood stump.

Its handle swept toward the sky
(Whatever that might signify);
Its mouth was dry as chimney clay—
And if it knew, it didn't say.

4
The White Stallion
(The Runaway)

A white horse came to our farm once
Leaping like dawn the backyard fence.
In dreams I heard his shadow fall
Across my bed. A miracle,
I woke beneath his mane's surprise;
I saw my face within his eyes,
The dew ran down his nose and fell
Upon the bleeding window quince. . . .

But long before I broke the spell
My father's curses sped him on,
Four flashing hooves that bruised the lawn.
And as I stumbled into dawn
I saw him scorn a final hedge,
I heard his pride upon the bridge,
Then through the wakened yard I went
To read the rage the stallion spent.

5
Old Hunter

The heart was ever a hunting thing
But the bones of men rebel,
So I'll rise no more to the whirring wing
Though the season's good for quail

When the moon lies cold on sedge
I'll draw my chair to the hear
Though the fox cries out to th
Old Buck keeps still in th

The Hound I'll hunt has
And a hungry star i
The hulking Bear I
Will bleed thro

7

Poem to a Mule, Dead Twenty Years

Traded by my father in a drunken rage
you died later in the yard of the processing plant.
I thought of you in the guts of hounds
circling the sedge, threading the trees at night
you, sly nibbler,
driving the fury along their veins.

No statues are raised to mules
(not even animal crackers),
but I would have it known
how once we commanded dead fields
and they answered, gold or green.

8

Old Barn

In this old barn much more than hay
    has gone to seed.
The harness hangs so still you'd think some hand
    would need
To set it right when times are slack,
    and Old Tom would
If he weren't dead. He'd clear the aisle too,
    if he could,
Cutting rank weeds that spring where
    his wagon stood
Brimming with hay, as if they sensed
    he'd gone for good.
(Weeds never dared to cross the fence
    like this before.)
No single hinge but squeaks too, like the
    swollen mice
That sift the hay above. No hand now to
    brush the ice
Away from troughs at dawn—and no need.
    Cobwebs fall
Ghostly, clear to the empty mangers in each stall,

9

And, under the ruined roof, some horse's ghost
Tramples the moonlight to keep out the
    stinging frost,
And make the peevish owl rattle
    the canted door.
When a barn goes, this is the way it has to die:
With a hayloft free to any bird passing by.
With a crib full of rats. With a well running dry.

Rural Scene: Without Wordsworth

No impulse threads this vernal wood
Winnowing evil out from good
Nor coils within the cypress knee,
Moralizing stone and tree.

The millhouse squats in quietude
Where undisturbed the owls brood,
And creaking in the autumn rain
The mill wheel rots, grain by grain.

All quaintness gone, no tourists come.
The shrunken pond is greenish scum
And underneath, the ripples hint
Of tooth and claw abandonment.

One gothic stump is sullen host
To tuneless frogs—instead of ghosts.
These pines are ringed by merely bark
To gird them for the coming dark.

II

Abandoned Plow

Whoever left this plow
to warp in wind and rain
(in a field of broom sedge now)
unhitched in dark despair—
and knowing he'd never return
to finish the furrow again,
left it: worn handles, beam and sweep,
for only the quail to keep.

A Small Elegy for a Poor Farmer

Earth, who turned his every crop
　　Into bitter weed,
Cover now the farmer up:
　　Fructify this seed.

2

*Five Poems as Homage
to Robert Frost*

The Invitation Holds

The poet said, "You come too,"
And having little else to do
That day, I climbed the pasture fence
To watch him rake the leaves away
From the mountain spring.
I never meant to stay
Except, perhaps, to pet the brindled calf—
But that was long ago.

You say, "What kept you so?"

He knew how not to sing,
Or, singing, took the minor key.
For all his stance, an angled tongue,
The twinkled eye
Behind the metaphor of stone;
He had the strength to sing alone.

"You come too," the poet said.
And so I came and tarried on,
And still his world unfolds.

The invitation holds.

One Patch of Snow

The way one patch of snow,
   Stubborn and alone,
Flake by flake lets go
   Before the raging sun,

Yet holds the slope as though
   It won't acknowledge flight,
Lends hope to one who knows
   The closeness of the night.

Burnt Farmhouse

The lonely chimney stabs the sky
And heart of every passer-by
Who stops to note the farmhouse yard,
The way the twisted oaks are scarred.

The martin gourds are hanging dumb,
The well has gone to greenish scum,
And where the barn is thick with dust
A toothless harrow turns to rust.

Each night the thicket seems to throng
Up closer to the scuppernong:
In moonlit rows there stalk about
Three homeless ghosts the fire drove out.

The Fallen Scarecrow

The way his scarecrow chose to fall
Between two young bean rows
(Wearing his cast-off hat and clothes)
With nothing near to make it sprawl,
No cattle, shoat or wind,
Has turned the old man's mind
(With nothing close at all),
Has charged his house with fright—
And left him counting through the night.

The Conspiracy

Here where deer cross over at dark
The pavement gives; it bears the mark
Of hunted hooves that scrape and thin
The road where snorting bucks plunge in.

And yellow sedge has leaped the fence;
It wears the mask of innocence
And, silent, gnaws the yielding tar,
Hiding the place where tunnels are

Mined by rain. Even ants conspire
To haul cement along the briar,
And live oaks thrust a levered root
That cracks the surface, foot by foot.

I should report this subtle crime,
And oh I shall, but in due time:
Let it be in another season
When I've lost all heart for treason.

3

A Mountain Sabbatical

Wild Grapes
(After Pushkin)

I will not miss the shy selfheal
shedding blue tears, nor the trumpet's flare;
I will not care when the yarrow fails
and autumn nears,

for I love wild grapes that bear
over rocks where white waters curl:
blue-black, cool, treacherous to pick,
more beautiful-scented than any girl.

Split-Rail Fence

The way a split-rail fence has failed
To hold this beauty back, old rails
Too tired, too gnarled and weather-maimed,
Itself too random to contain
Wild blooms that spill between and over
(Queen Anne's lace, blue grass, and clover)
To somersault down the mountain slope
Like water from the mountain spring,
Has stirred in me some secret hope
Not born of the buoyant spring,
Has cheered me over a road accurst
And slaked a deeper thirst.

Climbing the Falls
(For William E. Taylor)

First, you will remember the snake on the rock,
Headless and coiled to a question mark
Against the bloodless stone. Here,
   broken and cool,
The waters fanned its death and pooled
Under the bridge's pride.

Then, shoeless and young, we climbed the falls,
We two, between the greening walls
Of pine. Gray-lichened rocks we climbed
Or, hand and foot, through emerald slime
Until at last we stood upright
On the tall earth's bones.

                 Dizzied by height,
We danced on ashes of stone. We splashed
Like kids where granite ribs were washed.
I quoted Keats, and I remember that you
Were reminded of Twain. We left to birds
To say what neither could bend to words;
We let our shadows speak to the stone.

Then, in a shower of praise, it was down
The falls the safer way. On hands and knees
We fell, threading the scattered debris
Of broken glass, away from the roar
Of cleansing waters we'd climbed before,
Until at length on the last rock stood
To balance the falls and our drunken blood.

We laced our shoes by the question mark,
Breathing dead snake and the falling dark.

Reading Li Po in the Mountains

Reading Li Po in the mountains
   under the humpbacked shadow, bored,
I hear the phoebe sing of peach blossoms,
   of mulberry trees by a drunken road. . . .

Now the sky burns blue as a plum
   over inebriate pine
   over a crow turned crane—

Till my heart, a hunkering toad,
   uncoils like a silken skein.

The Encounter

It wasn't the pulse in root or bark,
No wild thing waiting for the dark:
Nor was it the whirr of startled wing
That gave me pause; yet some *thing*
Held me like a spell close by the clump
Of sedge where foxgrapes twined the stump.
So there, drunk with the musk, I stood
While thrushes rinsed the autumn wood.
Oh, I knew the things it was not
And tolled them one by one. But what
It *was* would give no further sign—
Or if it did, I couldn't divine
The hint, not with a thrush at ear.
Some spirit, say, nothing to fear;
A sound as though the earth could purr
Beneath the sedge, or at random stir
Some muted strand of rusty wire
To hum one note among the choir
Of birds—a note as yet untamed.
So circled by the wilds it claimed,
"Come out," I said, "and be named."

Pastoral

Under the sullen shadow of this mountain
  no pampered lambs go frisking;
Only the wind bleats at the door,
  breathing windfalls;
Here in the valley roots of nettle eat stone.
Haunted by owls, the gray barn dies,
  sumac and sedge tumbling its weathered walls.
A bubbling stream? Yes, polluted and dull;
And for nightingale, one crow, my familiar,
  humps on the burnt-over knoll:
It is against these I risk myself,
  and go on risking. . . .

4

A Bitter Season

The Guilty

*"The Police Chief reported that over 30 persons a week
confessed to the murder of Miss G."—News Item*

Riddled by guilt, they squat in holes
    Dimly lit, soured with sin;
Like sullen moles they snout headlines,
    Or wrinkled bats, begin

At dusk to flit through alleys, bars,
    Or tenement's abyss.
With bulging eyes they sorely sweat
    To scent what they confess.

They snuffle a gangrenous spoor
    Up stairs of dark intent,
Have access to the fatal door
    Which spews what they repent.

These are the beasts of neon kills,
    Who held, they swear, the ax;
Who skulk in dives, garrote for thrills—
    They specialize in sex. . . .

Now cry, "Kill me for the crimes I sow,
    Oh Christ, oh Mary kind;
That naked corpse you've hunted so
    Is rotting in my mind."

Jonathan Edwards

When Jonathan preached his flaming word
He stood up straight like an Eden sword;
When Jonathan prayed for Jesus' sake
Bones would rattle and graves would quake,

Stout old sinners with beards of hoar
Skinned their knees on the hardwood floor.
When he bent those Puritan necks
Wives forswore red ribbons and sex.

He wrung their hearts, he loosed their thews;
They jumped like spiders in the pews;
They bit their tongues and rolled their eyes,
Starved for a glimpse of Paradise.

Moppets confessed to ancient crimes,
Swooning away for weeks at times.
And when the church was cleared of smoke
Jonathan tallied the hearts he broke,

The ones who swooned, the ones who shook;
He walked right home and wrote in his book,
And totted up how well he'd scored—
Fell on his knees, and thanked the Lord.

My Son's Illness
(For Leslie)

My young and only son is ill.
Hugging a blue dolphin
he sinks in a white fever
    like the waters of a dream.
I think of princes sickening to toads.

The walls breathe out and in,
    a raspy accordion,
darkness rubbing like fur on the window.

At midnight
I float over a one-eyed zebra
a pride of mangled lions far below.

In the kitchen I curse the breathing of all
    appliances
until chilled by the deep freeze
I fumble my own pulse:

What if I have no second chance?

Estrangement

(For Jimmy)

I watch my son romping the sea,
    Small shadow haloed by foam;
A green tide coiled at his knee
    Hisses his tender bone.

Was there whisper of salt to blood
    Not meant for me on land,
Not heard because the serpent flood
    Struck at the dying sand?

Joyful among crustacean kin,
    He sprawls where fiddlers spar,
Then stares at me with dolphin grin
    Beside a sibling star.

The Green Stallion
(Suggested by Jung)

Why do I always dream of wild horses
    and never de Soto's windy plains?
Why do dream horses gallop my rickety house
    instead of the fabled pastures?

I hear their hooves thunder the attic
    and panic the mice:
I hear them snorting in the cellar,
    screaming as though trapped by fire,
    pawing the pantry as though bitten by mad
    dogs.

Stampeding the bannisters, they tremble the
    stairway.
Startled by mirrors, they spill old books
    from shelves and crash fruit from the table.
They nibble my curtains, and die.

I find them stiff in my bathtub,
   hear twitching hooves in the attic,
   rasping breath in the cellar.
They hang themselves from the chandelier,
   dripping blood on scattered books and apples.

And once I saw in a dream
   a green stallion arch through the second-floor
     window,
   its nostrils flared, its mane surprised;
I watched it writhe, green and dying,
   squandering red blood on the pavement's gray.

34

I Too Elpenor

I too Elpenor
know how it feels
to be the youngest of the band,
to be of least force
and own the weakest head
when ripe wine whirls in the mixing bowls.

I too have sprawled on the cool porches
a stone's throw only from Circe's bed. . . .

Therefore:
I know what it means
to rise at dawn
and fall, reeling,
into the pit among the towering dead

unwept for   and   unsung.

Afterwards

on the way back
from the deep woods
(the boy gone)

three martin gourds
writhed on the cross
under low skies

and dry sunflowers
(all of them)
turned dark heads
to the path
accusing her

The Dead Sea Scrolls

The Dead Sea Scrolls were discovered by
Muhammad adh-Dhib, "The Wolf."

At the end of the wolf's stone springs the Word.
The Qumran seed, cradled in caves, swaddled by
    flax,
(Two thousand years under the spiders'
    patience)
Breaks from shattered jars into the oppressive
    light
And putrid air of holy lands.

Marred by faction, blighted by scholarly lust,
Suffering the cyst of coin, the pustule of disbelief,
(Some hidden beside the privy wall)
Where bullets choir beneath a castrate sky—
Now "The War of the Sons of Light" and Isaiah
    prophesying anew:

Under the wolf's stone springs the psalm of
    praise,
Blossoms the lamb-white Word of God.

Soldier's Return

I saw them shun my face's scar
And I saw as I searched the street
Not one man worth the dying for
Nor one worth living to meet.

38

The Fist

Like that German in the story by Mann
my life, all of it, has been a closed fist.
Should I say, dear, that you turned fist to flower
    blooming finger by finger?
You didn't.

5

Poems Just for Fun

A New Apple

To see this new apple
   red against the round blue dish
   and neither Plato's appleness
   nor, in its flesh, the arms of Helen
   pointing to broken walls.

To see the fruit itself, I say,
   and neither swollen breasts disguised in dreams
   nor fated snakes coiled round its core.

To see the freshness of things, yes.
Ha!
Are there no seeds for poems here?

Two Verses after the Greek

I

THE PATIENT LOVER
(After an unknown poet)

I pleaded when you were a young grape;
    Laughing, you spit in my eye:
What answer now, Marcella,
    Old raisin wrinkled and dry?

II

FREE AND EASY
(After Archilochus)

As one fig-tree in a land of rocks
Feeds whole flocks of crows,
So freely Melanctha Rose
Diddles her dandy cocks.

Two Little Love Poems

I

POEM TO BE ENCLOSED IN A LOVE LETTER
Dear, you are so beautiful
I fear old gods may rise
to put on beastly disguises,
raping in feathers and fur.

(Such things once were.)

I have dreamed of great white wings
beating against buses,
Corridors rank with boars,
and once, I swear, that lucky bull
    with you astride
Triumphant among the quaking taxis.

43

II

LOVE POEM

        Yes,
how when you rise from your chair
arranging your dress
I breathe
        and
the room
(bookshelves blue walls oh shining air)
arranges itself
        around
           you.

Readings at Lake Como
(For Evelyn Thorne)

Over wine from A & P
Under a bright Matisse,
We read our poetry
Munching rye and cheese.

In a fog of metaphor
And syllables of praise
We dreamed our lines would shore
Unregenerate days.

And pledging Dylan's ghost
We made his records rage;
Applauded by a tipsy host,
Chanting page on page.

As the Matisse blurred
Our toasts went round and round;
We cursed the Abstract Word,
Obscurity and Pound,

Deplored the need to explicate
Sly Eliot's epigraph—
And I went out to urinate
And heard the Muses laugh.

6

Editorials

The Solitary Horseman

"Parents are advised against giving a child a rocking horse because it does not develop the group spirit."

I'll buy a horse for my young son
And help him on it. Whereupon
I pray he'll spur across the floor
And, solitary, leap the door

And paltry shrub. I'll hear one hoof,
Arrogant against the roof:
Then all below will see and cry,
"What bold rider usurps the sky!"

The Bleeding Men

We do not live in Astolat:
We cannot choose to bleed or not.

Each day we go forth bleeding men;
Each night our blood is that much thin.

The time is one of open veins
That drip in streets and clot the drains,

And money in the bankrupt heart
Is squandered now before we start—

Yet though the cheapened pennies flow
We learn to make our pulses slow.

The Painted Signs

I don't give a damn for all these painted signs
   that tell me JESUS SAVES
   and CHRIST IS ON HIS WAY.

Let there be laws against those great red wooden
   hearts
   that hawk God's love.
I can read.
(I read your barren hearts across this land.)

I would have shapely barns that shed a grace
   on all who pass this road;
   ungirdled pines like spires;
   and hayracks straight as steeples
   where shocks of corn are pitched like Aaron's
     tents
     beneath the thrush's song.

I would have shapely men and women
   to shoulder the morning skies . . . .

If you've the love your wooden hearts proclaim,
I say, Tear down these ignorant painted signs
   and let me read your eyes,
   only your blinding eyes.

Ladies Club Luncheon

The theme is anti-poverty
and the centerpiece is an old brogan
with its tongue out
like a starved hound's.

The work shoe blossoms
with wildflowers:
Queen Anne's lace, snakeroot,
the savagery of blackeyed Susans
dark as the hole in a Negro's shirt.

The chairman taps her glass with a silver spoon,
The speaker shuffling notes like kings and queens.

Something good will come of this!
Something good will come of this!

Dessert waits in crystal bowls:
Poorboy pudding.

When We Dropped the Bomb
(After John Hersey)

When we dropped the bomb on Hiroshima
   it roasted pumpkins on the vine
   and baked potatoes nicely under the ground;
   deep in the vaults the x-ray plates were spoiled;
   men became sterile; women miscarried,
   but sesame and sickle throve in ashes and puke.

When we dropped the bomb on Hiroshima
   the soldiers' eyes ran from their sockets
   and smeared like honey down patient faces;
   unnumbered thousands lay in the streets
    in vomit and died politely
    under the darkened sky.

When we dropped the bomb on Hiroshima
   the wounded crawled to Mr. Tanaka's garden,
   retching among bamboo and laurel
   fouling the exquisite garden, the pools,
   staining the pools, the delicate bridges
    arching . . .
   (No one wept.)

All day the young wife rocked her swaddled
    corpse;
  a burnt horse walked on the dying,
    trailing its entrails
  while Father Kliensorge scratched in ashes,
    seeking his melted Christ.

When we dropped the bomb on Hiroshima
  it worked; it was altogether good.

So we turned to Nagasaki.

Hearing War News

Hearing war news on the car radio
the latest bulletins of body counts
my beams piercing the hurtling dark . . .

a dog explodes under my wheels
and suddenly
the road is alive with small brown bodies
crawling away from legs or arms;
trailing pink entrails
   they fall
      into my quaking dreams.

7

Imaginary Epitaphs

Epitaph for a Meat-Packer

Here my meat is, clean and dressed,
Newly packaged and expressed;
On the day I'm resurrected,
Angels, stamp me *God-Inspected*.

Epitaph for a Garbage Man

All my life I carted junk,
Bits of bone, flesh that stunk;
Now that I am turned to slop
Will God take this garbage up?

Epitaph for a Beatnik Poet

Here lies Bogus, beatnik bard,
Who wrote obscenely by the yard;
May he get his just desert
Now that dirt returns to dirt.

Epitaph for a Munitions Maker
(After Ammianus)

Here rest the bones of old von Krupp:
Lie lightly on them, gentle earth,
So the dogs may dig them up.

Aunt Ella

Dear Aunt Ella, who warred with dirt,
Is laid beneath the dust, inert.
And now we pause and bring to mind
How all her pots and windows shined;

How forth she marched with deadly rag,
A brush her sword, a mop her flag,
To drive some mote beyond her door
That dared profane her sacred floor.

But now though dirt surrounds her room
Aunt Ella never lifts a broom:
If you would keep her, Lord, you must
Give her a mansion rife with dust.

8

The Groves of Academe

The Hanged Pazzi Conspirator
(A Sketch by Da Vinci, 1479)

Slouched under the wall
    by the window of the Borgello
      the bastard Leonardo

Sketched you dangling on air
    your neck twisted, so,
    your time publicly run out.

Then cruelly jotted your dress,
    splendid in death
    ("A doublet of serge,
    A blue coat lined
    With fur of foxes' breasts")
      item by item.

Where are they now, Bernardo Bandini,
    Your hangman,
      judges,
    the Medici you murdered?

You, whose black hose swing darkly,
    a pendulum
      in the mind of man.

The Beggars
(Brueghel, 1568)

Brueghel painted misery raw, and here
Five beggars lean to burn the viewer's mind,
Like five gross spiders. Dumb eyes a-stare,
Their goggle mouths are gaped like open
    wounds—

One head affects a bravery of red.
Truncated torsos twist on wooden pegs
And flourish symbolic furs. On menacing legs
Like crabs', one peers; one's feet are loaves of
    bread.

Our eyes, unless they blur with pitying,
Must vault this pain. They do, they run
These red brick walls to fields, and leap to seize
The green and tender prophecies of Spring.

Twilight Comes to Connemara
(In Memory of Carl Sandburg)

Let the shadows stretch over Connemara
A goat cough in the rising fog;
Let a wind from the blue-gray Smokies
    stir hemlock and laurel
    under Big and Little Glassy.
The Poet had said, "This is the place;
    we will look no further."

The singing Swede?
"He's long gone, oh, he's long gone"
and would have it no other way.

Set the green eyeshade by the Lincoln bust.
Let the guitar strings go slack,
the Havanas lose their aroma. . . .

Let twilight come to Connemara.

The Past

(With My Luck)

Sometimes, in spleen, on leaden days
When skies are overcast
And blues come wrapped in sodden haze
I yearn unspeakably for the past,
Those spacious times, remote and free,
Of the *Golden Hind* and Virgin Queen—
I long for a London spree.

Oh, to quaff ale with Nashe and Greene
Or sport with Kyd at the Triple Tun,
To conquer Ben in a bout of wit
And tup a voluptuous nun
(Reeling off sonnets, of course, between)
And wind up roaring at the Bull or Pit.

What rot! What unthinkable folly
Even to dream of Drake or Raleigh.
With my luck, in a lordly age
I'd be dropped in a sty to beg
Till peppered by fever or plague.
With my luck my nostrils would leak in the
    stocks,
I'd marry a drab with the pox
Or stab, in my cups, some noisome tart,
And go whining to Tyburn in a creaking cart.

After Plato, after Socrates
(To My Coeds)

After Plato, after Socrates
and the wintered wisdom of Saint Paul
you nod in golden assent.

You parrot my weakest clichés
in themes, filing the senses
down to a cold and puritan bone.

With red lips tight, your breasts turned stone,
you spurn the five sties
that hold mere women in thrall . . .

Yet the bell refreshes white bones:
that moment you rise
and go forth in all your April fleshes
under my leaping praise!

To a Pregnant Student

I could never make you quick; your sullen feet
Scraped in and out my door;
A stone beneath the waters of my wit,
You slouched, bovine and bored.

Aloof alike to Pope or Locke
You doodled on a page
As vacant as those sterile eyes,
Which only read the static clock;
(You cheated on the sly.)

But now some boy has tutored you
And found you wise, has turned the key
To rooms forever shut to me,
More secret than sea-chambers, famous in song,

Until, swollen with the knowledge you've put on,
    you rise
With what new meaning in those vibrant eyes.

Three Coeds Walk on the Grass

In shorts, their nakedness a nimbus there,
Three laughing girls ripple the shining air
   Beside the sparrowed halls. . . .

Lord, how the flesh falls from their lyric bones!
They walk, they dance upon themselves, these
   three;
While grasses groan to suck their melting thighs
And greedy earth buckles beneath the toes
   Where lilting shadows fall.

This raging sun will bore the sockets of their eyes
And heal their ragged names on every tree. . . .

   How soon their balanced bones will fall from
     grace;
   How brief and burning are their days
   Above the lawns of praise.

Commencement Day

Here in these halls of ransomed youth
The boards are washed, the colored chalk
Is boxed, and dead the practised talk;
Now windows clean as the edge of truth
Mope on the ordered, empty walks,

And silence settles on charted walls.
Where sunlight sweeps unlittered floors,
Swirled once a vertigo of life: Beowulf's troll
Would roar his pain. . . . Now Ahab's cursed the
    snowy whale
And Byron has tupped a final whore.

Soon mid medieval pomp, austere clichés,
Beneath those regimented palms,
To trumpets' blare across the sterile lawn,
The bridled young, decked in the harness of
    praise
Will heel the dull and castrate dons.